THE ADVENTURES OF SPIDER

THE ADVENTURES OF SPIDER

WEST AFRICAN FOLKTALES

RETOLD BY
JOYCE COOPER ARKHURST

ILLUSTRATED BY
JERRY PINKNEY

LITTLE, BROWN AND COMPANY
BOSTON   NEW YORK   TORONTO   LONDON

Library of Congress Cataloging-in-Publication Data

Arkhurst, Joyce Cooper.
    The adventures of Spider : West African folktales / retold by
Joyce Cooper Arkhurst ; illustrated by Jerry Pinkney.
          p.   cm.
    Summary: Presents six tales about Spider, including those which
explain how he got a thin waist and a bald head and why he lives in
ceilings and dark corners.
    ISBN 0-316-05107-1
    1. Tales — Africa, West. 2. Anansi (Legendary character) — Legends.
[1. Anansi (Legendary character) 2. Folklore — Africa, West.
3. Spiders — Folklore.] I. Pinkney, Jerry, ill.   II. Title.
PZ8.1.A7Ad   1992
398.24'52544 — dc20   92-444

                    10 9 8 7 6 5

                           WOR

                Published simultaneously in Canada
            by Little, Brown & Company (Canada) Limited

                Printed in the United States of America

Contents

To all the friends in Liberia and Ghana
who told me so many stories on so many moonlit nights.

IN WEST AFRICA people love to listen to stories. Sometimes at night, when the moon is high, everyone in the village comes out into the wide, clean place where people sit and talk. The last cooking fire has gone out, and the last jar of water has been carried from the river. It is a time to rest.

The moon is so bright that people can see each other's faces. The forest behind the village is tall and black, and full of night noises. Crickets sing and tree bears cry and tree frogs croak. Leopards and elephants are walking softly.

Inside the village, the little round houses stand in a circle. And inside the circle there is a great fire, and the people are cozy and happy. The women come talking and laughing. Their voices are soft and musical. Their long, brightly colored skirts sparkle in a lovely kind of night-way.

The men have been sitting under a shelter, drinking a drink that comes from the palm tree. Slowly they walk to the storytelling place. Their long robes swing from their shoulders like sails in the wind as they walk.

The children are playing with small fishing boats like their fathers' or they are playing hop-scotch or hide-and-seek. They, too, run toward the storytelling place, taking their younger brothers and sisters with them. Tiny babies, wrapped in wide bands of cloth, sleep safely on their mothers' backs.

Everyone sits in a circle. "Let us call the story-teller," someone cries.

And so the chief sends a messenger to call the one who tells stories best. Soon he comes. He is a tall brown man with a sparkle in his eye. He puts a low stool in the center of the circle near the fire. He stretches his long legs comfortably and sits down with his elbow on one knee. Then he looks far into the night, thinking which story he will tell first.

"Tell us a story about Spider," cry the children. "Yoo-oo-oo," answer the people, and that means they would like to hear it, too.

Everyone knows about Spider. He is a favorite person in the stories of West Africa. Maybe it is because he is just like a naughty little boy, who is full of mischief and yet loved by everyone. Maybe it is because he is like some people all of us know, and maybe it is because he is a little like you and me—or at least a tiny part of us sometimes.

Spider is clever and mischievous. He loves to eat and he hates to work. He plays so many tricks that he gets into a lot of trouble. But when he is good, he is full of fun.

We will pretend. We will sit by the fire and listen to the one who tells stories best. He will tell us how Spider came to be the way he is. And as the storyteller speaks, he will strike his stick upon the ground.

"Once upon a time," he will say. "Once upon a time—do you really believe it? Perhaps it is not really so, but this is what they say. Once upon a time . . ."

As he speaks, the people of the village will listen, listen with us.

How Spider Got a Thin Waist

MANY dry seasons ago, before the oldest man in our village can remember, before the rain and the dry and the rain and the dry that any one of us can talk about to his children, Spider was a very big person. He did not look as he looks today, with his fat head and his fat body and his thin waist in between. Of course, he had two eyes and eight legs and he lived in a web. But none of him was thin. He was big and round, and his waistline was very fat indeed. Today, he is very different, as all of you know, and this is how it came to pass.

One day Spider was walking through the forest. It was early morning and he noticed an unusually pleasant smell. He wrinkled his nose and sniffed the wind. It was food! Goodness! He had almost forgotten. Today was the festival of the harvest. Every village in the big forest was preparing a feast. The women were cooking yams and cassava, and chicken with peanut-flavored sauce. There would be fish and peppers and rice boiling in the great pots over the fires.

Spider's heart jumped for joy. His mouth watered. His eyes sparkled and he smiled brightly. Already he could taste the food on his tongue.

Now, of course, Spider had not done any of the work to deserve such a feast, and no one had invited him to come and eat. Spider had not planted yam or potato. He had not planted rice, nor gone to sea in a long boat to catch fish. For Spider did not like to work at all. All day he played in the sun or slept, and since it is not the custom to refuse food to anyone who comes to one's door, he could eat very well by simply visiting all his friends. In fact, he ate more than they did.

Now Spider was right in the middle of the

forest. Not far away there were two villages. Spider stood just in the middle, and the two were exactly the same distance away. Today each village would have a great feast.

"How lucky for me!" thought Spider.

But then he was puzzled. Since there were two dinners, he did not know which one he wanted to go to. That is, he did not know which would have the most to eat. So Spider sat under a breadfruit tree and thought and thought and thought. At last he had an idea! He could go to them both! Of course. Spider was so pleased with his good idea that he did a little dance right there and then.

But how could he know when the food was ready? He sat under the breadfruit tree again and thought and thought and thought. And then he had another idea. He did another little dance just because he was so brilliant. And then he did two things.

First, he called his eldest son, Kuma. He took a long rope and tied one end around his waist. The other end he gave to his son.

"Take this rope to the village on the East," he said to Kuma. "When the food is ready, give the rope a hard pull, and I will know it is time for me to come and eat."

And so Kuma went to the East village and took the end of the rope with him.

Then Spider called his youngest son, Kwaku. He took another long rope and tied it around his waist, just below the first one.

"Kwaku, take this rope to the village on the West," he said, "and when the food is all cooked, pull very hard on it. Then I will come and have my fill."

So Kwaku went to the West village, carrying the end of the rope with him.

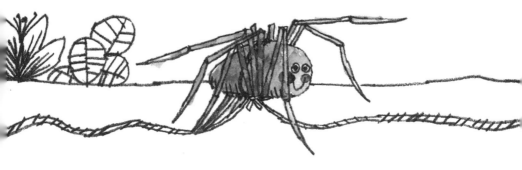

My friends, can you imagine what happened? I don't think so, so I will tell you. The people in the East village and the people in the West village had their dinners at *exactly the same time.* So, of course, Kuma and Kwaku pulled on both of the ropes at the same time. Kuma pulled to the East and Kwaku pulled to the West. The ropes got tighter and tighter. Poor, greedy Spider was caught in the middle. He could go neither east nor west, nor left nor right.

Kuma and Kwaku could not understand why their father did not come, and they pulled harder all the time. And something was happening to Spider. The ropes squeezed tighter and tighter and his waist got thinner and thinner. Kuma and Kwaku waited until all the food was eaten. Then they came to look for their father. When they found him, he looked very different. His waist-line was thinner than a needle! Spider never grew fat again. He stayed the same until today. He has a big head and a big body, and a tiny little waist in between.

Why Spider Lives in Ceilings

ONCE upon a time the rainy season came to the forest, as it must come every year. But this time there was more rain than ever before. Nobody had ever seen anything like it. At night the water fell with a roar like thunder. In the morning it beat against the branches of the trees and tore their leaves from them. It pounded against the thatched roofs of the villages and rushed about the footpaths. Little girls set pots under the sky to catch the water, and ran back slipping and sliding. The small, friendly rivers became deep and wide, and covered the sides of their banks. During the darkness the people fastened their doors and did not even look outside, for they could hear nothing but rain, rain, rain.

The animals in the forest, too, were frightened

by all the water. Hare could not find meadows of grass for his dinner. Elephant could not walk through the trees to chew the young branches. Tortoise could not crawl slowly along the earth to catch insects; and Spider, who had been too lazy to plant his farm or to set his fish traps, had nothing to eat at all. Worst of all, the great Leopard, who hunts at night, was hungry, and had to stalk the forest during the day.

One afternoon, after many days, the rain stopped. Spider set out at once to look for

something to eat. He went down the wide path that led to the river. Leopard was hunting, too, with a hungry look in his eye. He walked quietly on his four soft feet along the path that led to the river. That is how it happened that Spider and Leopard walked right into each other.

Now usually, Leopard loves a fat and juicy supper. He never thinks of anything as puny as Spider. But today he thought even Spider would taste good, and so he stopped to chat and tried to look friendly.

"Good afternoon, Mr. Spider," said Leopard. "How do you fare in all this wet weather?"

Now Spider was lazy and very naughty, but he was not stupid. He knew at once that Leopard's voice was much too sweet.

"I am well, Mr. Leopard, but I am in a great hurry," he answered. And with that, Spider jumped behind a great palm leaf, and Leopard could not find him, no matter how he tried. Leopard was so angry. He roared a roar that echoed against the hills. He sharpened his claws and his eyes turned green.

"Never mind," he thought after a few minutes, "I will go to Spider's house. I will hide behind his door and wait for him to come back. Then I will eat him, and if he brings any food, I will eat that, too."

Leopard went up the path from the river. He went into Spider's little house, which was made of banana leaves. There he made himself into a round ball. He put his nose on his great paws, and sat down to wait.

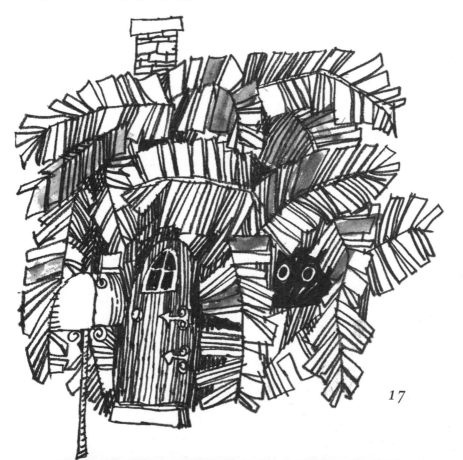

Haven't I already told you that Spider was not stupid? He guessed exactly what Leopard would do. And so he took some time to think how he should handle the matter.

First, he went to the river and caught some fish left in the traps by people. Then he went to a farm and ate a cassava. For it is the custom that a hungry man can help himself to as much food as he needs, and no one will mind.

When he had enough to eat, Spider spent the afternoon looking for all his friends. He stayed away from his house as long as he could. Finally, it began to get dark. The sky filled with clouds, and once again the rain began to fall. At last Spider *had* to go home. So he went up the path that led past the river, and near his little house made of banana leaves.

Spider looked at the earth to see if Leopard had left any tracks. Hc listened to see if Leopard made any sound. He saw nothing and he heard nothing. Still, he knew the ways of Leopard, and he decided to try something else.

So he kept walking down the path, humming to himself, just as though he were thinking of nothing. Suddenly he cried out.

"Ho! My banana-leaf house!"

Nobody answered. Everything was silent. Spider walked a little nearer. Still there was silence. Nobody said anything.

"That's funny," said Spider loudly, "my little house always answers me when I call her. I wonder what is wrong."

Once again, with all his might, he shouted, "Ho! My banana-leaf house. How are you?"

And from deep inside the house came a small high voice. "I am fine, Mr. Spider. Come on in."

Then Spider burst out laughing.

"Now I know where you are, Mr. Leopard, and you shall never catch me," he said. And with that he ran as quick as a flash through the window and up to the highest corner of the ceiling. Leopard could not catch him although he tried and tried. Spider was warm and dry and safe in the ceiling. I suppose that is why he decided to live there. And he is living there still.

How Spider Got a Bald Head

I HAVE already told you, and you have already seen for yourselves, that Spider was very full of mischief. He was often naughty and always greedy. But sometimes, in the bottom of his little heart, he wanted very much to be good. He wanted to be kind, and he wanted to help someone.

He tried so hard, but his appetite almost always got in the way. In fact, that is why Spider has a bald head to this day. Would you like to hear how it got that way?

One morning, Spider awoke early in his little leaf house beside the small river. The sun was bright and the sky was as clear as a bell. Spider smelled the good breakfast his wife Aso was cooking. He felt good all over. He wanted to do something to help someone. Who could it be?

Quite suddenly, he remembered his old mother-in-law. Of course! He would help the old lady plant her rice. It must be hard for her to walk through the forest to her farm every day carrying her food on her head, he thought. Spider told Aso of his plan, and she was very happy. She gave Spider a special gift to take to her mother.

So it happened that Spider set off to the farm of his mother-in-law. It was a great distance, and as Spider walked, the sun grew hotter. He crossed the slim long bridges that reached over the rivers and walked down the small pathways that cut between the tall grasses, and climbed past the house of Pepperbird who lives on a hill. When at last he reached the farm of his mother-in-law, he was already quite hungry.

He found the old lady bent over the earth planting seed.

"Good morning, my mother," said Spider.
"I have come to help you plant the rice."

Aso's mother was overjoyed. She thanked
Spider and showed him just where to start
planting.

"When we have finished," she said, "we shall
have lunch. I know you are very fond of beans,

my son, and so I will cook the very best ones I have." And she took a great cooking pot and filled it with beans and onions and peppers and tomatoes and meat. Then she went to a small kitchen not far from where Spider was working, and put the pot on a fire to cook. With that, she went to another part of the farm to work.

For a long time everything was just fine. Spider worked on one part of the farm, and the old lady worked on another part.

After a time the beans began to send out a wonderful smell. The longer they cooked, the better they smelled. The sharp spicy smell rose up out of the pot and floated right across the field, and into Spider's nose.

How Spider tried not to notice it! He tried to look away from the big pot. He tried to face in the other direction. But somehow, he seemed to be getting closer and closer. In fact, each time Spider dug a hole and planted a seed, he seemed to take a step closer to the pot of beans. It almost looked like a little dance. Spider dug a

hole, planted a seed, took a deep breath, and jumped sideways—toward the pot. He tried ever so hard, but he couldn't stop himself. Finally, he stopped trying, and simply ran over to the cooking pot.

Spider's heart pounded. He looked around to make sure that no one was looking. He snatched his hat off and put some of the beans in it with a long spoon. And then he ate them. Mmmmm! They were good. Once more he looked all around. No one was coming. Quickly he ladled the beans into his hat. He piled them higher and higher, until the hat was almost full of boiling beans.

Now in another part of the land not very far away, many people were planting rice. Suddenly a flock of rice birds flew down upon the field and began to steal away the seeds. The people shouted and threw stones at them. The big birds rose up in the air. They flew straight into the little kitchen. There stood Spider with his hat full of beans.

Spider heard a great commotion. He saw a large number of birds flying around him. Just behind them came a crowd of people. What on earth could he do? What a disgrace to be caught with a hat full of beans. There was no time to hide them and there was no time to run away. So Spider threw his hat on his head, and, of course, you can guess what happened. The beans began to burn. Spider started to shake his head. He jumped up and down and ran around in a

circle. All the time the beans got hotter and hotter. And the hotter they got, the harder Spider shook his head and the higher he jumped and the faster he ran.

The people all noticed the way Spider was acting, and asked him what was the matter with him.

"I'm doing the hat-shaking dance," shouted Spider, and his head moved faster and faster. "I must go to my father's village, for it is the time of the hat-shaking festival."

"What is that?" asked the people. For they had never heard of the hat-shaking festival.

"The hat-shaking festival, the hat-shaking festival," cried Spider. "It comes every year. I must run right away, because my father will expect me."

And Spider ran down the path that led into the forest. But all the people ran after him, because they wanted to know all about the hat-shaking festival.

All the time the beans were getting hotter

and hotter. At last, Spider could stand it no longer. He snatched off his hat, and beans, onions, meat and peppers scattered everywhere. Everyone roared with laughter, for they saw what had happened. Spider's head was as bald as an egg. Not a hair was left on it. Spider was so ashamed that he asked the grass to open for him so that he might hide, and the grass took pity on him and hid him. That is why Spider still likes to walk through grass, and, even today, he is still bald.

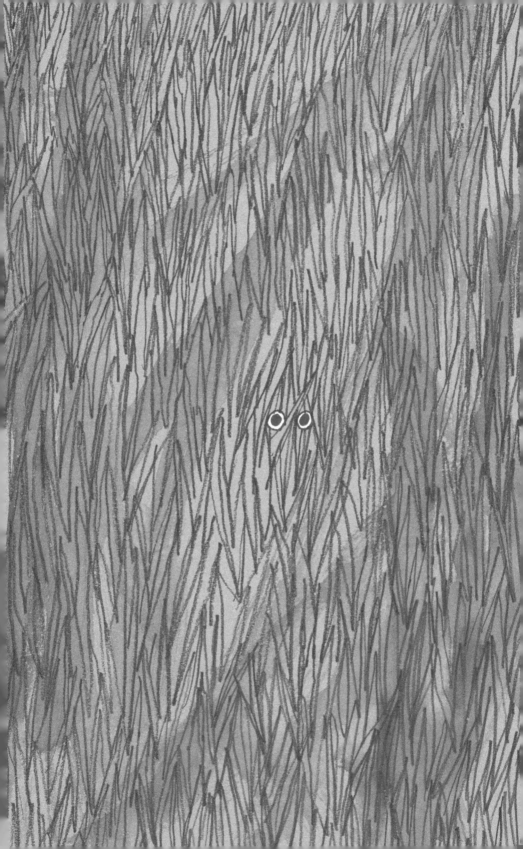

How Spider Helped a Fisherman

IN THE VILLAGE of Akim there was once a fisherman who worked very hard. Every morning he gathered his nets into his long boat or set his traps in the river. Sometimes, even at night, the fisherman went far out into the sea, and when he returned he mended his nets and cleaned his boat. Spider noticed how hard the fisherman worked. But he also noticed how many big fish the fisherman brought to his house each evening, and what a feast the fisherman's family had. Spider was determined to find a way to get some of the fish for himself, and so one day he went to see the fisherman and offered to help him.

Now, of course, Spider did not intend to do any work. He thought he could play a trick on the fisherman and get all the fish he wanted without having to work at all.

But the fisherman knew all about Spider. He knew that Spider was greedy and lazy and always up to something. Yet, when Spider asked if he could help him, the fisherman said, "Of course, you can. I will be very glad to have you help, Spider."

The people of Akim all laughed. "What a fool is the fisherman!" they said. "Spider will take all the fish and the fisherman will do all the work."

But the fisherman only smiled. "You will see," he thought to himself.

On the first morning when Spider came to help, the fisherman said to Spider, "Now let us discuss the way we will go about things. Someone has to do the work and someone has to get tired, so we will take turns. One day you will be the one who gets tired, and I will do the work.

The next day I will be the one who gets tired, and you will do the work."

"Do not talk in long sentences," answered Spider. Only talk about what we will do today."

"Very well," replied the fisherman. "Today we will make traps to catch the fish. I will make the traps and you will get tired."

"I get tired?" shouted Spider. "Indeed not. I will make the traps, and you will be the one who gets tired!"

For Spider hated to get tired more than anything.

"Very well," said the fisherman, "if that is what pleases you."

And he lay down on the ground as though he

were very tired, while Spider made all the traps.

The following day the fisherman said to Spider, "My friend, today we must set the traps in the river. Yesterday you made the traps and I got tired. Today, we'll change around. I will set the traps in the river and you will get tired for me."

"Never!" shouted Spider, who hated to get tired and wanted to get some fish. "I will set the traps myself, and you will get tired."

And so Spider set the traps in the water while the fisherman lay down on the bank. Spider bent over for a long time, putting the traps deep in the water. After a while his back began to ache. All the while the fisherman lay on the bank. He watched Spider working. And while he watched he moaned and groaned and rubbed his head and rolled about as though he were very tired.

"My oh my oh my!" he cried. "I'm *so* tired." And then the fisherman went to sleep.

Well, on the third day the fisherman said to Spider, "Surely we must have a change today. It is only fair. I shall collect the fish from the traps and you will be the one who gets tired."

Now, you know Spider was planning all along to eat some of the fish.

"Do you think I am a fool?" he shouted. "What makes you think I want to get tired?

You will get tired and I will collect the fish."

"If you insist," answered the fisherman. And he lay down on the bank of the river again.

When the people of Akim walked past the river, they saw Spider busily gathering fish and the fisherman lying on the bank looking very tired. He moaned and groaned even louder than the day before, but this time he did not go to sleep. He kept his eyes fastened on Spider. So poor Spider did not get any fish at all.

On the final day, the fisherman said to Spider, "Today I really mean what I say. I will take the fish to market and you will get tired."

"Nonsense!" said Spider. "I will never agree to get tired. I will carry the fish to market and you will get tired."

And so it was, even up to the last day. Spider carried all the fish to market. The fisherman walked behind him, huffing and puffing as though he were indeed very tired. When they reached the market, Spider put the fish in a big pile. Then the fisherman sat down beside them. When people came to buy, they paid the fisherman, for was he not the only fisherman, and did not the fish belong to him?

When all the fish were gone, the fisherman gave Spider four coins, one for each day he had worked. Spider saw that he had been tricked instead of tricking the fisherman. He had very little of the money and none of the fish. At first he was angry, and then, as he was in the habit of doing, he simply burst out laughing at himself.

"Next time I will be the winner," he said. And he went merrily back to his little house among the banana leaves.

One who plays tricks himself may be tricked if he is too greedy.

Why Spiders Live in Dark Corners

SPIDER lived in a house made of banana leaves with his wife, Aso, and his two sons. Behind the banana-leaf house was a garden. In the garden Spider and his wife and his two sons planted yams and corn and tomatoes, bananas and lemons and oranges. When the rain came every year, the garden grew beautiful and Spider and his family had plenty to eat.

Every day Aso cooked rice and vegetables and meat and peppers into a big stew. It was delicious, and Spider ate until he could eat no more. You might have thought Spider would be satisfied, but of course he was not. He wanted to have even more good things to eat. I am afraid he wanted to eat most of the time when he was not sleeping.

"What can I do?" Spider asked himself. "There are so many good things in my garden, and yet I can eat only half of them. I wish I could think of a way to have more."

So Spider sat in his garden and thought. At last he had an idea. He told his wife he was not feeling very well and that he was going to see the village magician. The magician knew many things and could tell what would happen next month or next year. After a while Spider returned, and when Aso asked him what had happened Spider told her that the magician said he was *very* sick, and that very soon he would die.

Aso and her sons were sad, but Spider only said, "Since I am going to die soon, you must make a place to bury me. I want you to put it here, just next to the spot where the tomatoes are growing."

For Spider loved tomatoes best of all.

When Aso had dug a deep hole for Spider's

burial place, Spider said, "Now, I want you to put in some spoons and knives and forks, and some cooking pots, so that I can feed myself when I am in the next world."

And so Aso and her sons put spoons and forks and knives and cooking pots into the grave.

One day, very soon after, Spider pretended to get sick and die. He lay very still and closed his eyes, and tried to stop breathing. Aso and her two sons shed many tears and put Spider in his grave just beside the tomato patch. Spider stayed in the deep grave for several days because his family had a fine funeral, and many people came to mourn for him. They brought food and sang funeral songs and played the funeral drums.

When it was over Spider sat up happily in his grave. He did not mind spending the day there, because he loved to sleep anyway. And when night fell, can you guess what Spider did? Very quietly he lifted the cover of the grave. He looked about to make sure that everyone was in bed, and when he saw that all was safe he crept

out, very slowly. Sometimes the moon was so bright that Spider could see everything in the garden. He quickly picked several of the very best tomatoes. Then he pulled up some of the best yams. He cut off some green, juicy peppers and pulled up a few big onions. Then Spider crept into the chicken yard and plucked himself a nice fat chicken. When he had everything he wanted, Spider went back into his deep grave. He cooked a grand feast, and ate all night long.

Now it was not long after that Aso and her sons began to notice that something was happening to the garden. Every morning some of

the best tomatoes and yams were missing. They wondered who could be stealing from their garden. So Aso thought of a clever way to catch the thief. She brought a great pile of straw. Out of this she built a man that looked just like a real man. Then Aso got a bucket of soft, sticky beeswax. She covered the straw man with a thick coat of sticky beeswax, and when she finished she set the man in the middle of the tomato patch.

That night, as soon as everyone was asleep, Spider crept out, as usual. He was just about to pluck a big juicy tomato when he saw a man standing in the middle of *his* garden. Spider was so angry he forgot all about trying to be quiet.

"Who are you?" he shouted. "What are you doing in my garden?" But instead of explaining himself, the man only looked at him.

"So! You won't talk, eh? Where is your tongue?" asked Spider. "Get out of my garden at once."

But still the man said nothing. He only looked at Spider and stood still.

"Do you think I am playing? I will teach you a lesson," screamed Spider, and with that he hit the wax man as hard as he could with his right hand.

Ooof! His hand stuck fast in the beeswax. Spider could not move it though he pulled very hard.

"So," he screamed, "you are trying to be clever. I'll show you."

And he hit the wax man with his left fist. And that stuck, too. So Spider was stuck to the man with both hands.

"What is this? You are really too much," cried Spider. "Do you know who I am? I'll teach you a lesson."

And with that he gave a mighty kick to the wax man. What do you think happened? Why, his foot stuck fast, and he could not move it.

"Haven't you learned yet? Well, I'll give you another kick." And Spider kicked the wax man with his other foot, but it, too, stuck.

Now Spider was stuck hand and foot to the wax man. He began to get a little frightened. Still, he tried again.

"I am stronger than you," he shouted. And he gave the wax man a tight squeeze, and his stomach stuck fast to the wax man. "I will win this yet," said Spider and he butted the wax man with his head as hard as he could. And, of course, his head stuck fast, too.

The next morning Aso and her two sons went

into the garden to see whether they had caught the thief. Imagine their surprise when they found Spider stuck to the wax man from head to foot. At once they understood everything. They pulled Spider down and took him to the chief to be judged a thief. Everyone knew who the thief was then, and the people in the village laughed at Spider and made up funny songs about him. After a time, Spider was so ashamed of himself that he ran up into the darkest corner of the ceiling to hide. And he has lived there ever since.

How the World Got Wisdom

NOW, WISDOM is another word for good sense. Nowadays there is wisdom everywhere in the world, but there wouldn't be any at all if it hadn't been for Spider's accident. Would you like to hear a story about it?

When the world was very new, Nyame, the Sky God, gave all the wisdom in the world to Spider, and told him to do whatever he wished with it. Of course, Spider wanted to keep it all for himself, and so he put it in a huge clay pot and covered it up tightly.

"How lucky I am to have all this good sense," thought Spider. "One day I will become a king, for I will be the only wise man in the world. I

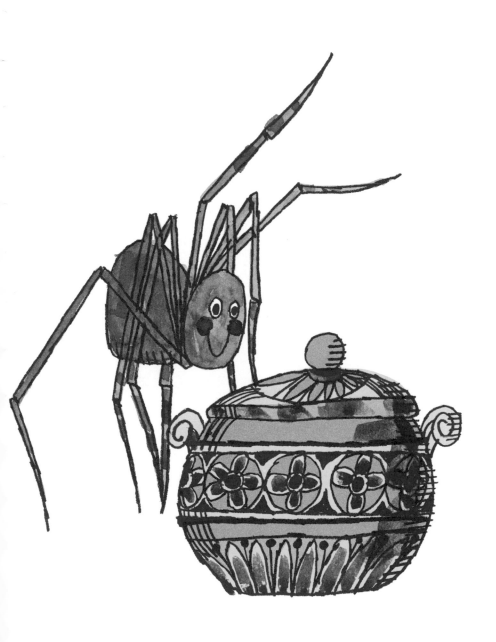

must hide it carefully, where no one else can see it."

Spider ran through the forest as fast as his eight legs would carry him, looking for a place to hide his pot of wisdom.

"Where are you going?" asked the Tortoise.

"Where are you going?" asked the Hare. "And why are you in such a hurry?"

But Spider didn't answer. He just kept running, looking for a place to hide his wisdom before somebody saw it and took some of it away from him.

"I know what I'll do," said Spider to himself.

"I'll hide my wisdom in the top of the tallest tree in all the world."

At last he found just the tree. It was a great silk-cotton tree. At the bottom its roots came up above the ground and they were wide enough to hide an elephant. Its smooth trunk was wide enough for Spider's whole house. At the top the branches spread out like an umbrella, and they were covered with soft silvery leaves, and a fine gauze that looked like cotton. "It's the perfect hiding place," cried Spider. "No one will be able to climb it, because there are no branches near the ground."

So Spider went back to the place where he

had left the pot of wisdom, and carried it to the foot of the great tree. Now, the silk-cotton tree is very hard to climb, for its outside is as smooth as a finger. But Spider was sure *he* could climb it. For one thing he had more legs than almost anybody else. People have two and animals have four, but Spider had eight.

Spider tied the pot around his neck with a piece of strong rope, so that it hung right in front of him. Then he made ready to climb. He put his two top legs around the trunk of the tree as far as they would reach. He put the next two legs around the top of the pot, two more around the bottom of the pot, and the last two under the pot. Spider pulled with his two top legs, and pushed with his two bottom legs, and held the pot with his four middle legs. My but the pot was heavy! After all it contained all the wisdom in the world. Little by little, he began to go upward. Spider was feeling very pleased, when suddenly he slipped. In fact, he fell all the way back to the ground.

"Dear me," thought Spider. "I have eight legs. Surely I can climb this tree."

So he started again. He hugged the tree as tightly as he could, and pushed and pulled with all his might. The pot was *so* heavy, and his two bottom legs just couldn't catch on under its weight. But this time, his luck was no better than before. He fell right back down to the ground. Spider was getting warm. And I'm afraid he was getting angry. He decided to try once again. So he pushed and pulled harder than ever. But the same thing happened. No sooner did he get off the ground than his middle leg slipped. Then his right upper leg slipped and his

left top leg slipped and his right bottom leg slipped, and BOOM! Down came Spider, pot and wisdom and all right on the ground again.

Now all this time, Kuma, Spider's eldest son, had been watching. "Father," said Kuma, "I have an idea. Hang the pot behind you instead of in front of you. Then you will be able to climb the tree."

When Spider heard this, he knew that Kuma had some wisdom too, and that he did not have all the wisdom in the world to himself. This made him so angry that he threw the pot to the ground. It broke into many pieces and the good sense poured out in all directions. It made such

a noise that people came from everywhere to see what it was. Old women came from the market. Men came from the farms, little boys came from their games, and little girls ran out of the round houses. And when they saw the wisdom pouring out of the pot, they all reached down and took some of it. Even the animals got some. They spread it all over the world. In India and Spain and Panama, where it is always hot or where it is always cold, everybody has some wisdom. Because there was plenty to go around. Plenty for you and plenty for me.